Mel Bay Presents

HAMMERED FIDDLE TUNES

by Rick Thum

Traditional American Fiddle Tunes Played on the Hammered Dulcimer

Cover image © Larry Ulrich Photography
"Autumn at Glade Creek Grist Mill"

Cover design by Ferd Bienefield

A recording of the music in this book is now available. The publisher strongly recommends the use of this recording along with the text to insure accuracy of interpretation and ease in learning.

Visit us on the Web at http://www.melbay.com — E-mail us at email@melbay.com

Dedication

This book is dedicated to my loving wife LuAnn. Thanks for your encouragement.

Thanks to my children Rian, Nathan, and Erica,
for putting up with all the practice and commotion at our house.

A **Special Thank You** to all of those who helped on this project,
Renee Poirier, Carole Bryan, Angela Oberkfell, Robert Howard, and Rich and Alex Usher.

Contents

Introduction to
Rick Thum

Music has been a major part of my life from a very early age. As a small child I carried a stack of 78 rpm records instead of a security blanket. "Camptown Races," "Polly Wolly Doodle," and "Shoo Fly" were just a few of my favorite tunes. My poor mother must have gone crazy listening to these tunes played over and over everyday. Tin cans and pencils made an early drum set for me. A cookie tin and tomato stick formed a crude banjo with rubber bands as strings. In seventh grade I got my first real instrument, a guitar. I taught myself to play a few songs and soon formed a band. My high school and college years were supported by playing rock and roll guitar and drums with several local bands. After college I tried to stop playing and got a real job. The lack of music in my life was unbearable, so I joined a local church choir playing 12-string acoustic guitar.

Sometime in the fall of 1989 I saw and bought my first hammered dulcimer. It was love at first sight. Although guitar was fun to play, it lacked a certain freedom of physical motion. Playing drums gave me this motion but lacked the expression of notes. The hammered dulcimer combined the best of both instruments, freedom of motion as on the drums, and musical expression as on the guitar. It didn't take long to figure out how to play and after lessons with such fine teachers as Kendra Ward-Bence, Cathy Barton, Ed Hale, and Jim Hudson I found myself deeply involved in the world of the hammered dulcimer.

In 1994 I placed first at the Southern Regional Dulcimer Contest. In 1995 I placed third at the National Championship at Winfield, Kansas. I have shared stages with *Mike Seeger, The Tony Rice Unit, Steve Kaufinan, Norman Blake,* and *Bryan Bowers* and opened for *John Hartford, Norman & Nancy Blake,* and *Leo Kottke.* At home I am the founding member of the *Cabin Fever String Band* and travel across the country playing solo and teaching at music festivals.

Teaching hammered dulcimer has become a regular part of my full-time job. I own a mail order business called *Mail Order Music* which caters to hammered dulcimer players' needs. I also own and operate my own independent record label, *RT Audio.* While the hammered dulcimer is my main area of focus, selling, repairing, teaching, and playing musical instruments of many types has now become my living. I have been blessed with the opportunity to make my love my work!!

The Recording *Hammered Fiddle Tunes*

Hammered Fiddle Tunes is a collection of traditional fiddle tunes I found to be most popular when I was first beginning to play the hammered dulcimer. The hammered dulcimer is front and center in the mix with guitar and bass backing. Bluegrass-style banjo is used, to trade leads with, on a few of the songs. A second dulcimer was recorded in the background playing chords only. The result is a lively rendition of some very popular tunes for the hammered dulcimer.

About This Book

This book is based on the assumption that you have a working knowledge of your instrument. All of the songs can be played on a standard tuned 12/11 instrument. I will show some of the techniques important to my style of playing. Understanding a certain technique is not necessary to being able to play these tunes. It merely helps you to be able to play them in the style presented on the recording.

How to use this book

Fiddle tunes were written to be danced to. Most tunes contain eight measures in the A part and eight measures in the B part. Each part is to be played twice, i.e., A A B B and then repeated as a block in this format as many times as the dancers need. The last measure of the A part may need a full four beats because the first measure started right on the one beat. It may only need three beats on the last measure when going to the B part because the B part starts with pickup notes that equal one beat. "Old Joe Clark" is an example of this. The music is written to show this. You must play the song in rhythm connecting these parts as if they were one measure.

Hand Patterns

You will not find tablature showing hand patterns or which note to hit because I believe that you will end up using the best hand pattern for you. I try to alternate hands as much as possible and to cross over a bridge with the hand closest to the crossover. I also try to play as horizontally as is possible. Sometimes a vertical hand pattern works out better, but for the most part your playing will be more accurate and smoother if you play horizontally.

Where To Start

How do you know where to start a piece? Let's say we are in the key of G which has one sharp. The sharp will appear on the music next to the time signature. (Fig. 2) When only one sharp is there you are in the key of G. The first or lowest G that is on the staff (Fig. 2) will be the G that is on the bottom right of the key of G on your dulcimer. The broken lines in Fig. 1 show the area that is the key of G on your dulcimer. X marks the note on the dulcimer (Fig. 1) that is shown on the staff below (Fig. 2). You will then play the rest of the music in relation to that first note.

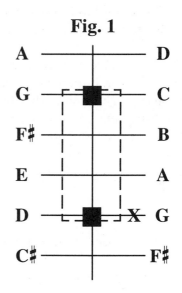

Fig. 1

Fig. 2

You will do the same thing for songs written in other keys. The key of D has two sharps next to the time signature. Find the lowest D on the staff. In this case it is the D right below the lowest line of the staff. This note will be played at the bottom right of the D scale on your dulcimer just as the G was. All other notes are played in relation to this note.

When a song is written in a certain key (say G) and the first note is a pickup note (say D) that is lower than the lowest G on the staff, that note will usually be played on the bass bridge straight across and up from the G. (Fig. 3)

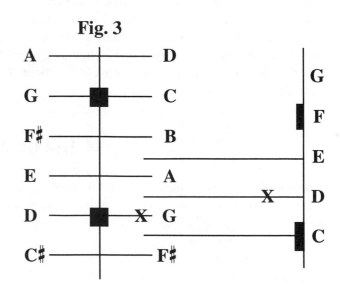

Fig. 3

Embellishments

Fiddle tunes are really simple melodies played over and over again. It is up to the player to add embellishments that make them interesting and alive. Throughout the book I will explain or write out a certain embellishment as an example of what can be done to the tunes. The real trick is to learn several of these embellishments and then to use them alternately or to mix them together. They can be used with the melody or as a replacement for the melody.

The Drone Technique

The drone is used in old-time music and fiddle tunes to add energy to the playing style. Old-time claw hammer or frailing style banjo also uses the drone note. The banjo is set up so that the player's thumb will hit the fifth string open as a drone. This drone sound is one of the sounds that really makes the fiddle tunes sound as they should. It is a style I use throughout the recording. I will not write out all the songs with their drone notes. "Golden Slippers" and "Home Sweet Home" demonstrate this method at length. You should then be able to add this embellishment to almost any song.

A drone by definition is a note added repeatedly to a song without changing the melody. The right hand plays the melody for the most part, while the left hand adds the drone note.

The idea is to get the melody reduced to all quarter notes. The right hand will be playing the melody as quarter notes while the left hand is droning quarter-notes at a softer volume than the melody. Yes, in reality that means that each hand is really playing eighth notes. The effect you are trying to get is that you are hearing the melody instrument with an accompanying instrument. That means the listener will hear the melody notes as quarter notes backed up or accompanied by drones played as quarter notes.

When an eighth-note run appears, as in "Golden Slippers," you must use your left hand on the melody line for the appropriate melody note. Yes, it will be played instead of a drone. The eighth-note run does not leave room for playing the drone note.

The best note to use for the drone is the fifth tone of the scale in which the song is written. In the key of G, the drone will be the D. In the key of D the drone will be the A. The fifth tone appears on the dulcimer directly to the left of the first tone of the key. It is straight across the center bridge to the left of the first note.

Other notes can be used for the drone. Trial and error will show you what works and what does not. I call it the *droning technique* because, by definition a drone is one note that does not change. This can get boring real fast. Changing the note will make the song more interesting.

Here is one good rule for changing the note. Drone the fifth until your melody goes up **past** the third tone of the scale of the key of the song. When it has passed the third tone, move your drone up the left side of the bridge to the next marked bridge. This is the fifth of the next key or the first of the key you are in, but an octave higher. Stay on this drone until the melody goes down **past** the third tone of the key you are in. (Same note that triggered the change going up.) You will then return to the drone you started with, which is the fifth tone of the scale of the key of the song. Sounds pretty confusing!! Look at the drone example written out for "Golden Slippers." Play what is written and you will be following the rule above.

Chords as embellishments

The chords are shown above the staff for each song. These chords can be used for accompaniment by another instrument such as a guitar, or as the basis for finding embellishment notes to add to the melody. I am assuming that you know how to find and use chords. They are a very powerful tool in embellishing a song.

Golden Slippers

Written by James Bland, 1879
Arrangement by Rick Thum

Below is the same song using the drone technique. Remember the right hand plays the melody, the left hand plays the drone. **The drone note should be played softer than the melody note,** which is for the most part the right hand. Start with your right hand and alternate hands. Two notes together are played with both hands. The next note is played with the right hand and you begin alternating again (ie., R L R L R L R L). For a more detailed example of how to develop the drone technique turn to "Home Sweet Home" and follow the three examples.

This is a different version of the B part. There are two different endings.

Home Sweet Home

Traditional
Arrangement by Rick Thum

To learn the droning technique, first learn the melody. Try to play all quarter, half, and whole notes with the right hand. In this case, the entire song can be played with your right hand. The next step is to turn the entire song into quarter notes as shown on the next page.

A.

B.

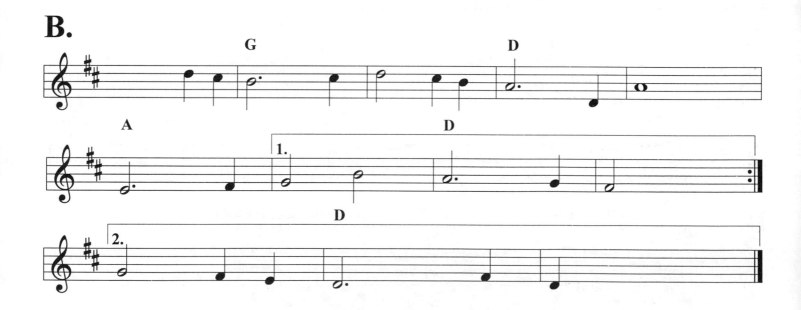

Home Sweet Home

Traditional
Arrangement by Rick Thum

In this version we have reduced all notes longer than a quarter note into quarter notes. When a note longer than a quarter note is reduced, the first quarter note of that reduced set should be played louder than the remainder of the set: i.e., a half note will be played as two quarter notes – the first one loud, the second one softer. The second note is a "filler" note, sort of like a back-up instrument adding to the melody which is out front.

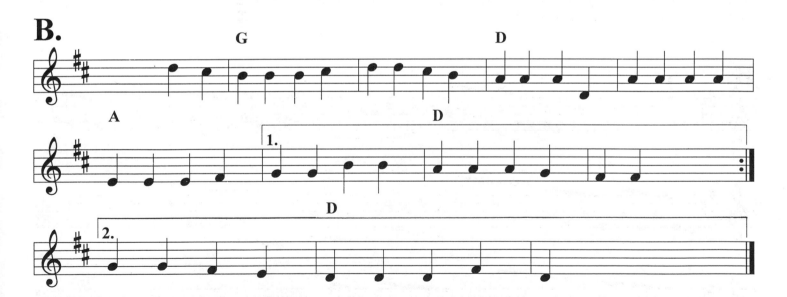

By hitting the A on the left of the center bridge with your left hand after each of the notes above are played, you will get a droning effect that will make the song get up and dance. The next page shows this song with full-drone technique. You will be using two notes for the drone.

Home Sweet Home

Traditional
Arrangement by Rick Thum

This is the full written-out version using the droning technique. The second note in the second measure is played with your right hand and then you alternate hands from then on. The same in the B part. This is an embellishment technique and will not be written out for each song in the book. It can be used in just about any song.

By hitting the A on the left of the center bridge with your left hand after each of the notes above are played, you will get a droning effect that will make the song get up and dance.

The Meeting House

Written by Rick Kuethe
Used with Permission
Arrangement by Rick Thum

The three-note chord on the end is played one note at a time, very
quickly. Play it from the lowest to the highest.

11

The three-note chord on the end is played one note at a time, very
quickly. Play it from the lowest to the highest.

Missouri

Written by Mike Dappert
Used with Permission
Arrangement by Rick Thum

A.

B.

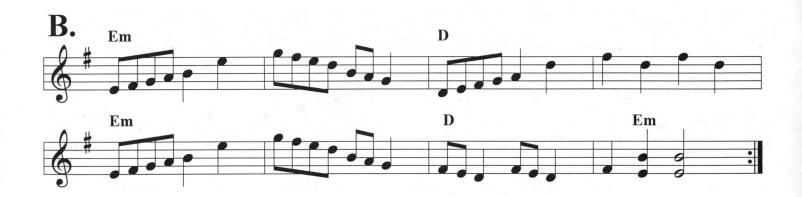

The A part below is an alternate part using a drone as embellishment. This time the hand pattern will be different. You will play R, R, L, R, R, L, etc. The drone note is played with the left hand. It is the second eighth note in each pair. The melody notes are played with the right hand. The drone note actually replaces one of the melody notes. The eighth-note runs, as in the fourth measure, are played with alternating hands, starting with the right hand.

A.

Soldier's Joy

Traditional
Arrangement by Rick Thum

The above version is the way that I first learned to play "Soldier's Joy."
Below is the more widely accepted version.

Ragtime Annie

Traditional
Arrangement by Rick Thum

Syncopated Embellishment

You have probably noticed an embellishment that has a syncopated sound. Syncopation comes from accenting a beat other than the first or third beat of a measure. Below is a lick I first learned from Kendra Ward-Bence. It gives a syncopated feel to the music. Practice this line as a drill and get used to how it feels. Begin with your right hand and alternate your hands for each note. This means your left hand will have to go up to play the B and your right hand will go over to the bass bridge to play the D. These notes make up a G chord. Accent or stress the high note in each phrase. In this case, it is all of the Bs.

Any three notes can be used to play this pattern. You will find that the three notes usually are the notes of the chord backing the song at that point in the melody. The melody notes are then used to replace the chord notes in their proper place to give you both the melody and the back-up notes. Below is the first line of the B part of "Ragtime Annie" using this method of embellishment. The C part also uses this technique. Practice the line above and move the pattern to other places on your dulcimer. With practice and some adjustments, you will find this to be a useful embellishment.

The next page gives you the B and C parts of "Ragtime Annie" with this syncopated pattern. Listen to the available recording to help you hear how it should sound. You will also hear it in "Golden Slippers," "Soldier's Joy," "Liberty," and "Circle Be Unbroken."

Ragtime Annie

Alternate Part
(with syncopation)

Arrangement by Rick Thum

This is a repetitive pattern. It starts with the right hand and then keeps alternating hands. The extra notes are embellishments that are rooted in the chords. The melody notes must be played louder than the embellishment notes. When you get this up to speed and really comfortable you will find that you can do this in other songs.

Whiskey Before Breakfast

Traditional
Arrangement by Rick Thum

A.

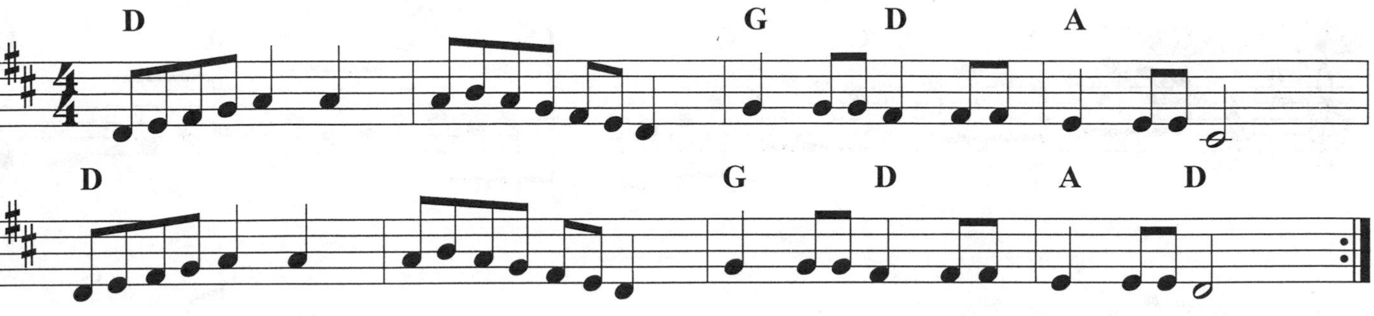

B.

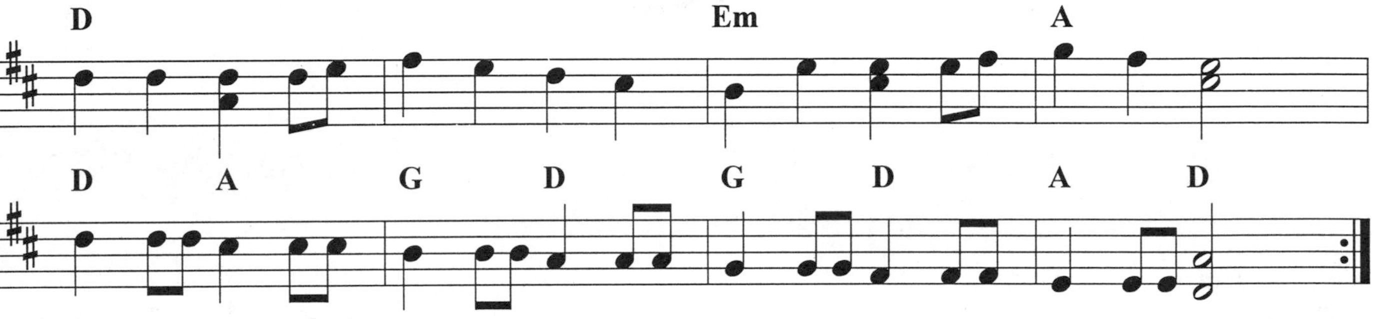

This is an alternate version of the song. Mix up the various versions.
It makes the song more interesting.

A.

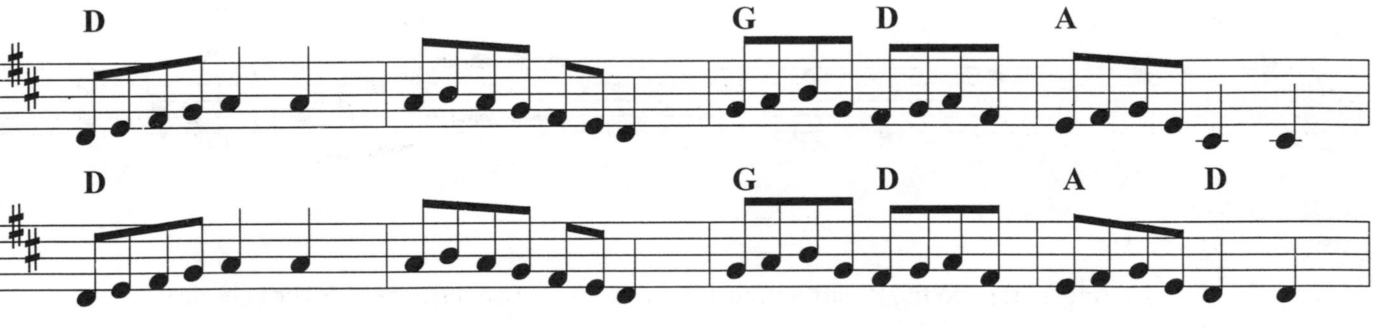

B.

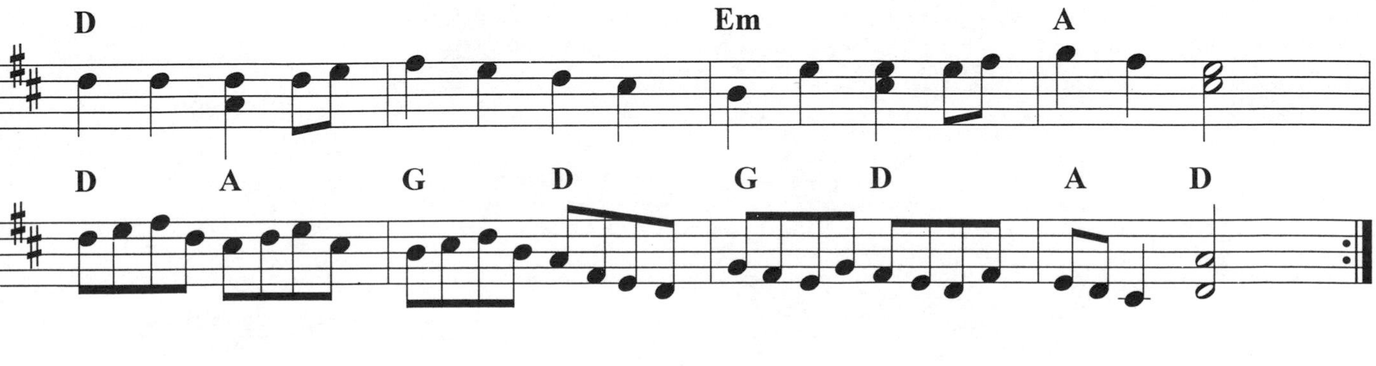

Blackberry Blossoms

Traditional
Arrangement by Rick Thum

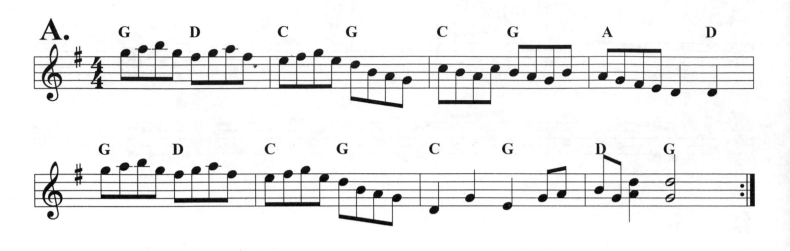

Adding a drone to the B part will really add life to it. Use the note of B for your drone.

Circle Be Unbroken

Traditional
Arrangement by Rick Thum

This song can use both the drone technique and the syncopation technique to make it come to life.
Use the notes of the backing chord and play them for the duration of the melody notes being replaced.

Old Joe Clark

Traditional
Arrangement by Rick Thum

A.

B.

The droning technique will add life to this song. Use the first note of each part as the drone note until two notes are played together. Then use the embellishment note of that two-note chord for your drone.

Country Dance

First Dulcimer Part

By Ferdinando Carulli (1770-1841)
Arrangement by Renee Poirier

Country Dance

Second Dulcimer Part

By Ferdinando Carulli (1770-1841)
Arrangement by Rick Thum

Petite Valse

First Dulcimer Part

By Dionisio Aguado (1784-1849)
Arrangement by Renee Poirier

A.

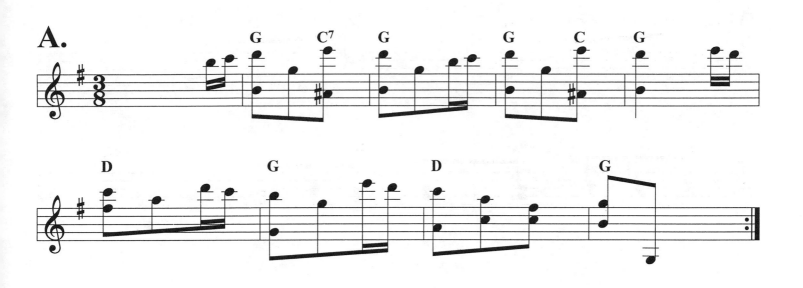

B.

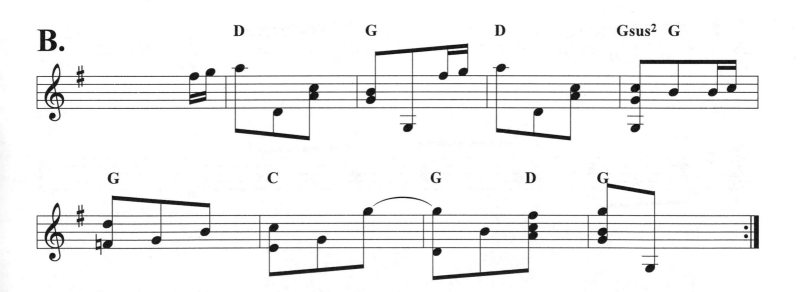

The three-note chords are played one note at a time, very quickly, from the lowest to the highest.

Note: This part was played on a Masterworks Chromatic Dulcimer. Not all dulcimers
will have the high E that is used in this song. Replace it with a lower octave E.

Petite Valse

Second Dulcimer Part

By Dionisio Aguado (1784-1849)
Arrangement by Rick Thum

A.

B.

Flop Eared Mule

Traditional
Arrangement by Rick Thum

Alternate version. Mix up: play version one, then two, then play parts of each mixed together.

The first two quarter notes in the A part can be replaced by a roll. You can also apply the drone technique you learned earlier. It fits best in the B part.

Liberty

Traditional
Arrangement by Rick Thum

Once again the measures above with all quarter notes can have the drone technique applied.

Alternate part using the pattern taught in "Ragtime Annie." The high note of each measure, which appears three times in each, should be accented. Start this phrase of music with your right hand and alternate hands throughout. The F♯ and the D are found on the left side of the center bridge; the A is on the right side of the center bridge. The next two measures just move up one note and play the same pattern.

Seneca Square Dance

Traditional
Arrangement by Rick Thum

This tune is usually played in the key of G. I chose to do it in D so it will fit the medley
with "Liberty" and allow for the key change up to G and back.

A.

B.

This song changes keys on the recording. To change keys just remember the hand pattern you are using and move it to the
same place in a different key on the dulcimer. Remember the key is the scale made by playing the eighth notes that fall
between two marks on the bridge. I call it playing in a diatonic square. To change keys just play the same hand pattern in
a different square.

A.